Swing Trading Strategies:

Learn How to Profit Fast With These 4 Simple Strategies

Table of Contents

Introduction..6

Chapter 1: The Mindset of a Trader...............9

Chapter 2: The Sector Rotation Strategy.....20

Chapter 3: The 4-Hour Chart.......................48

Chapter 4: Trading Fakeouts........................73

Chapter 5: Momentum Trading...................84

Conclusion..91

Additionally, the information in the following pages is intended only for informational purposes and should thus be thought of as universal. As befitting its nature, it is presented without assurance regarding its prolonged validity or interim quality. Trademarks are mentioned without written consent and can in no way be considered an endorsement from the trademark holder.

Introduction

Congratulations on downloading '*Swing Trading Strategies: Learn How to Profit Fast with These 4 Simple Strategies*' and thank you for doing so.

Many people view swing trading as more of a fundamental approach to investing in the stock market. Unlike with day trading where positions are never held for more than a single day, swing traders can conceivably hold their positions for up to several days or even a week or more; some may even hold them for a month.

Still, this is not a clear picture of what swing trading actually is. It is a form of trading that sits right in the center of two other popular trading mechanisms, day trading, and trend trading. The day trader needs to make super fast decisions and may only hold his assets for a few seconds before selling. Trend traders, on the other hand, are usually in the market for the long haul. They could conceivably hold their trades for months at a time. Swing trading is a blend of these two very different trading styles.

To be successful as a swing trader, it is important to know how to choose the right stocks to invest in. Ideally, you'll want to look for large-cap stocks, which tend to be the most actively traded on most exchanges. In this book, you'll learn how to ride the waves in one direction and know when to get off and collect your rewards at the end.

In the following pages you'll learn:

- How to develop the mind of the trader

- The 'Sector Rotation' strategy

- How to use the 4-hour chart

- What to do with trading fakeouts

- How to execute momentum trading

There is a lot you can learn before you even get started. Keep in mind that no one knows everything there is to know about trading the markets so see this as your first book among many. Here we hope to lay the groundwork from which you can then catapult yourself into a whole new world of profits and hopefully to a whole new way of making a living. With that said, let's get started.

Happy Trading!
There are plenty of books on this subject on the market, so thanks again for choosing this one! Every effort was made to ensure it is full of as much useful information as possible, please enjoy!

Chapter 1: The Mindset of a Trader

There is a good reason why trading is not for everyone. Statistics show that the majority of those who attempt a career in trading is not successful. This leaves us with a burning question...what is the cause of so many failures? Is it because they lack experience? Is it because of the intensity of the trade itself? Or is it because they don't have the right knowledge?

The answer is probably yes to all of those and the answer could also be no. Every day, thousands of traders enter the market; some win and some lose. We all know exactly what happens when we win and make a pretty good windfall, but how we react when we lose is another matter entirely.

Ask yourself, what do you do when you lose or make a poor investment choice? Some people may get discouraged, blame their losses on the volatility of the market and declare it as a waste of time. Another may also get discouraged and want to quit but, the next day they somehow find a renewed experience and are ready to try again. But the true trader will see the loss as a reason to ask more questions and do more research. Yes, they will be disappointed by their losses but, rather than let that loss be a stumbling block, they will use it instead as a stepping-stone. They will view it as an opportunity to revisit their data, reevaluate their position and find out what went wrong. In essence, they will use it as a learning opportunity and see it as becoming a better trader in the future.

Yes, the loss may have been a result of a lack of knowledge, limited experience, or even just bad decisions but, in a trader's mind, the reason for losing a trade is not as important as how they react to that loss.

To be able to do that, a good trader must learn how to keep their personal feelings completely out of the trading process. When you are emotional, it can taint your perspective of trading and affect your judgment. Traders must have an almost mechanical approach to every decision they make.

While all traders are in it for the money, the best ones are in it for the thrill of the game. They are not just following the charts to see whether they are going up or down but, are equally interested in perfecting their skills of analysis with every decision they make. They view everything as a real learning process.

When you trade you must make decisions quickly and be willing to stick to them and follow through with everyone. Each time you look at the charts, graphs, stocks, and other data, you may have only seconds to decide to get in or out of the market, there is absolutely no time for emotional involvement.

This means you need to be mentally stable, but many would be surprised to learn that you also need to be in good physical condition as well. They do not understand that good physical conditioning can actually support your mental acuity. Eating well, getting good physical exercise, and maintaining healthy habits actually supports your mental faculties, which could easily impact your choices when it comes to making good trading decisions. People who have poor health may not realize how their physical condition could have an adverse effect on their decision-making process.

Trading is more than the ability to watch the numbers going up and down on a graph, it's about the psychology behind those numbers.

All those squiggly lines, bars, and shapes represent decisions that individuals make to enhance their interest in a particular stock so the trader must have the ability to get into the minds of others and predict what he or she expects the majority of people will do. Then the trader needs to determine where he or she will best fit in that picture and make their decisions accordingly. At the same time, a trader must also create an escape hatch that will help them to get out of a trade to cut their losses whenever a decision he or she makes goes wrong.

The mind of the trader must be able to handle stress as well. It is difficult to watch the rise and fall of the market and realize that you missed your window to get in or out at the right time. One bad decision in this regard could really ruin your life in the future. It is said that patience is a virtue but, it can also be a lifesaver for the truest and most successful traders.

Just as you would work to hone your physical body, the best traders also put a lot of energy in developing their skills and sense of discipline. The more you practice in this area, the easier it will be. The ability to identify a good stock, learning how to time the market, and predicting price movements are just the public demonstration of the psychology behind the art of trading.

You also must be willing to be a lifelong learner. When it comes to navigating the many instruments you can trade in, you will always find that there is something else you need to learn. This means you must have humility and be willing to openly admit when you don't know something. The moment you become over-confident and think you've mastered a certain skill you can pretty much bet that something will come along to knock you back down a peg or two. You'll either lose your shirt or you'll be beating yourself up for a missed opportunity.

There is a very specific art to swing trading and learning everything you can about the market is tricky. Being able to do a proper analysis and make the right decisions is only a reflection of what's going on in your own personal mindset. To be a good trader, one that is successful most of the time, depends on how well your mind works and how well you know and understand people. Every trade you make will be a reflection of that mental acuity that you have developed. If you for any reason that feel you are weak in this regard, don't despair. It just means that now is the time to start sharpening your tools so you're ready to get the best that you can possibly get out of your trades.

How to Find Potential Trades

One of the most important factors in successful trading is mastering the ability to choose the right instruments to the trade. Many do not realize that there is also a certain psychology to making the right choice. It is just as important to identify not just those stocks that will move, but also where to look for them. No matter how good you are at trading if you can't identify the right instruments to trade you won't get very far as a trader. You need to be able to identify those stocks that have enough movement to generate a profit for you and those that have the volume to match it.

When choosing a good trading stock it is not enough to pick something you just like and can get excited about, but you must also be able to put your personal feelings aside and focus solely on the numbers. While a good product is definitely a plus, much more is involved in choosing the right stock. You want to see more than a movement, you must also be able to identify the direction its next move will be. To do this, you should look for those stocks that have a strong risk/reward ratio.

You can identify these stocks of the current news items circling around them, their numbers will show them, usually moving up or down more than 2% even before the market opens, and they generally have a lot of unusual premarket activity to go along with it.

Keep in mind that not all stocks are ideally suited for trading so as a trader you will need to be willing to evaluate them on a case-by-case basis. Just because a stock has a high trade volume does not necessarily mean that it is a good choice for swing trading and the fact that it has a low trading volume does not preclude it from consideration. Only after careful analysis can you determine whether a stock is the ideal trading instrument. You need to look for those stocks that are performing outside of the average to decide if it's the right choice for you.

There are many factors that must be considered when trying to choose the right stock. It is easy to think that you can just go by the books and get the results you want, but that would put you at a disadvantage. The numbers can reveal a great deal about a particular stock, but sometimes just relying on your human instinct can be a better gauge for making the right choice or even knowing just where you should look to find the right stock for your next trade.

Making the right choice will depend on a combination of your personal knowledge of the market, the skills you have honed to perfection and your natural instinct. Missing any one of those factors could definitely cause a major problem for anyone looking to get into swing trading.

Chapter 2: The Sector Rotation Strategy

One of the most effective strategies in swing trading is sector rotation. It has been proven to be an excellent means of generating profits with the least amount of risk. There are a few things you must keep in mind when you're practicing sector rotation:

- Market Timing — when the market is going down to avoid buying any stock. This includes purchasing any type of ETFs or sector funds.

- You will divide the market up into specific sectors. Some of these sectors will perform better at different times than at other times.

- Evaluation of each sector using both technical and fundamental analysis.

- Rotate the sectors every month to capitalize on your profit potential.

We'll go through each of these phases in more detail in the next section.

The general idea behind sector rotation is that each sector may perform differently depending on the time of the year it is. So, while some sectors may perform well in the spring others may have their time in the limelight in the summer or winter seasons.

Your goal is to identify those stocks and when you have the best chance of generating a profit from them. To do this, you will need to break down the different stocks into sectors first and do a detailed analysis of each sector. Once you've chosen the sector you want to trade in, you will have to do a separate analysis of each stock within that sector to narrow down your options for trading.

There are a number of websites that are perfect for listing the different sectors and the stocks contained in them. For a quick reference, you can go to Finviz.com to get a listing of the ones that are performing the best. However, if you are just beginning, it may be better for you to do the analysis and ranking yourself so that you can get a better feel for how they are divided up.

The general gist of sector rotation is being able to move your money from one industry to the next in an attempt to glean the most out of the market at any given time. As you go through the different industries, it is important to keep in mind that the past performance of any particular stock is not a guarantee of future success. With that thought in mind, there are four different stages of market movement you must understand.

- **Market Bottom:** This is the point where the prices of a particular stock begin to decline, creating an all-time low.

- **Bull Market:** This is when the market begins to rally and come back to life.

- **Market Top:** This is the point when the market reaches its maximum potential and begins to flatten out.

- **Bear Market:** This is when the market starts its long trip to the market bottom.

There are also four stages of the economic cycle that are important to always keep in mind. Remember that these cycles usually trail behind the market cycles by at least a few months.

Full Recession

When there is a full recession, it can be a difficult time for many businesses. The country's GDP will have been retracted for several quarters, interest rates will have dropped, and consumer expectations will have seriously declined. There are few industries that fare well during this period of time, however, those that are cyclical tend to do better. The technology industry and industrial markets also seem to do well in this type of economic climate.

Early Recovery

In this phase, things are beginning to improve economically. Consumers will begin to expect more from the market and industrial production is starting to see a gradual increase. By this time, interest rates have already bottomed out and aren't expected to fall any further, and the yield curve (the line that plots the interest rates used as a benchmark for measuring the economic climate) is starting to rise. Industries that tend to do better in this type of economic cycle are usually the industrial sector, those that supply basic materials, and towards the end of this cycle, you might even see potential in the energy sector.

Late Recovery

During this economic phase, you will see a rapid increase in interest rates and the yield curve will begin to flatten out. Consumer expectations will begin to drop and the industrial industry will level off. Industries that fare better during this phase include energy, staples, and services.

Early Recession

During the earlier recession, things will begin to decline for everyone. This is a period when consumer expectations will fall to an all-time low, the production industry will start to fall, and interest rates will be at their highest. The yield curve will neither be rising or falling but instead will remain flat or maybe inverted. The industries most likely to perform well in this economic climate will be services, utilities, cyclical, and transports.

In most situations, financial markets will try to predict the economic climate in the future. They may make predictions as far ahead as six months, putting the market cycle ahead of the economic cycle. So, when you hear news reports about the economic condition of a particular stock it may be well ahead of the current situation. So, a stock may be struggling at the time, but the news reports may already be talking about its recovery.

This gives you a pretty basic understanding of how the different sectors can be divided up and how to choose which ones will be best suited to trade. Even with this basic overview, you can quickly determine which industries are most likely to succeed during the different stages of the economic cycle. Once you've determined which market cycle and economic cycle you're in, it will be much easier to determine which companies you are more likely to take a risk on and give you a better chance at earning a profit.

There are two different ways you can earn profit through sector rotation. First, you can buy when the sector is trending upward and sell when the trend is beginning to fall backward. This is a basic rule of thumb, buy low and sell high. This concept is pretty easy to understand, but it is not always easy to detect. If you're like most people who enter the market, deciding when a price has hit its peak so you know when to get out is not always easy. The same can be said for determining the point at which the price has hit its lowest point possible.

If you're not completely sure how to go about it, there are several free websites you can refer to that will give you their viewpoint on whether the price is maxed out or not. Whatever you do, it is not a good idea to guess at what stock will perform well. Flash crashes are quite common and to be forewarned is to be forearmed.

You can also use charts to predict market movements. Beginners usually will start with something simple like the Simple Moving Average (SMA) to help them to make their decisions. Listed below are a few ways you can use to help you decide which way to go.

Identifying the Bottom of a Sector

It is difficult to determine when a sector has reached the bottom or the top of its cycle. However, if you choose to use the SMA-350, (that's the Single Moving Average over 350 sessions) to determine the market you could probably get a pretty good picture of when the market will begin to make its next dive.

Historically, stock prices have generally been seen to hit bottom after six months into a recession. As we've already pointed out, once several quarters have closed the negative growth of the GDP is a strong indicator. However, identifying these periods is not always that easy to see. Usually, if you rely on the six-month in a pattern most of the action has already taken place. As the expression goes, hindsight is always 20/20. However, there are other strategies that can actually be very useful when it comes to detecting a bottomed out stock.

Nothing could be better than getting into the market when a stock has reached its bottom point. That's when you can buy at the lowest possible prices and then ride the wave all the way to the top. To do that, you just have to watch and observe the averages before it reaches that point. If the averages have experienced a large break that falls below the previous low, it is a signal that you need to follow that stock and observe what happens next. There are several things that can happen. If the average experiences some type of reversal it could be an indication that a double bottom is developing.

You can also keep a close eye on the stock's volume. This measures the amount of activity going on with that stock; which is basically how much buying and selling is actually happening. If you observe a heavy volume going either up or down it is an indication that the buyers and sellers have a pretty strong conviction. If there is a lot of volume moving up, then there is strong support from buyers and if you see a lot of volume moving down it indicates that there is a great deal of support from sellers.

Looking at economic numbers can also tell you a great deal about a stock. The market will experience a decline after the negative news reports appear in the media. You need to think of the press as a reflection of the psychology of the moment. When you begin to see repeated headlines discussing how bad the economy has become, it is usually a sign that the majority of people have developed a very negative attitude towards the market and many investors will be moving out of their positions running for a safer haven as a result.

Consumer Confidence Index

Right after the market has bottomed out, consumer spending will begin to increase showing that consumer confidence has improved. This can be observed when they begin to spend more money and businesses start to see an increase in their earnings.

Managers' Index

This measures the economic health of a sector. When the consumer's confidence index and the manager's index both have hit rock bottom they will begin a steady rise that will continue for several months. You'll usually see this when you're observing the movements of the manufacturing and service sectors and indicates that they are beginning to expand and grow again.

High Yield Bonds

The high yield bond spread consists of bonds from companies who are at a high risk of default. To draw investors that they can borrow from, they will offer to pay a higher interest rate as an incentive. When the usual lending standards begin to relax you will notice the amount of interest for these types of loans will start to drop. This is a sign that banks and other financial institutions are prepared to take on more risk showing that the economic conditions are beginning to improve.

Copper Prices

Many will also look at how the price of copper is moving. It is usually a good measure when showing the strength or weakness of the overall economy. Since copper is so widely used in products like pipes, radiators, electronics, and other technological devices, observing how its price moves are a pretty good measure in determining consumer demand. If you notice that the price has bottomed out, then you can pretty much determine that the demand for those products is also pretty low. However, if there is still room for the price to drop further it's a good chance that there is still some demand for the production of many of the products that use copper.

Ideally, you want to enter the market when the prices have reached the bottom and are starting to climb upward again. It means that there is an increase in demand and prices are about to rise once more.

Being able to identify a market bottom is a key factor for any trader. It requires looking at a variety of different factors that involve both technical analyses as well as understanding the psychology of the masses.

You could choose to rely entirely on the numbers, but you would only be cheating yourself. However, when you use all the different indicators you can unlock the key to a host of profit potential.

Detecting the Trend

Another strategy you can use in sector rotation is detecting the trend. Sometimes this can be much easier than identifying the top or the bottom of a market cycle. Some traders use the metric SME-50 (50-day Single Moving Average). Here if you see the stock price has moved up more than 3% above the SMA-50 it is a good time to buy in, but if you see the price has dropped more than 3% below the SMA-50 that's when it is a good idea to sell.

Of course, once you get the hang of this type of analysis, you can always adjust your metric. You don't need to stick to the 3%

threshold and may prefer to use 1% or 2%. The key is to find a measure that will work best for you. Generally, if you plan to hold your stocks for a longer period of time, it is better to use a higher percentage and if you plan to sell after only a short period of time, use a lower percentage. You should also adjust your formula to reflect the frequency of the trades you want to make as well.

Identifying market crashes are also important. This tells you when it's a good time to get back into the market. There are also several indicators to help you to determine this as well.

The RSI (14) is a measure showing whether or not a stock has been overbought or oversold. The RSI usually oscillates between 0 – 100. A stock is considered to be overbought when the value increases to above

70 and it is oversold if the measured value is below 30.

What Should You Buy

Now that you have a good idea of when to get into the market and the type of market you want to trade you're only halfway there. In each industry, there may be hundreds, if not thousands of stocks to choose from so narrowing down your search for a good stock can be a little tricky. The stocks you choose will depend on a number of varying factors, some may be within your control and others may be out of your powers of influence.

You will have to consider your level of experience, and the amount of capital you want to invest. The method you chose to try to pick your stocks should be a part of your permanent trading plan and should be adjusted as your experience and knowledge in this field grows. Keep in mind that stocks will have different levels of price movements and velocity. Some will move very slowly and others will move very quickly. All of these factors will help you to decide which is the best choice for you.

Before you even begin to choose stocks, however, it is important for you to determine the kind of risk exposure you can handle. Your strategy should be created with this foremost in mind. You want to reduce the amount of capital at risk and limit your exposure, but at the same time, you want to earn a sizable profit. The best way to accomplish that is to make enough, right decisions that you can generate a steady stream of profit for yourself.

Keep your process simple. Whatever strategy, it is that you're using start by trading a single stock and then sit back and observe what happens. Every stock has its own personality and habits. The more you understand them the easier it will be to anticipate its movements. Look at the charts at different times throughout the day to determine when it moves and how it responds to external stimuli. Think of it as developing a love interest. You want to know all its little quirks and habits. In time, your relationship will solidify and you'll be able to predict its movements with surprising accuracy. You won't get it right every time, but the number of wrong predictions will eventually begin to diminish. Once you've reached a level of consistency, you can move on to get to know other stocks in your particular industry.

One important thing you need to remember. Once you've started a trading plan, do not change it while you have a stock in play. Once you've pulled out and the market is closed, you can then look back and make some adjustments to your plan. This way you will know the exact results of your decision and you'll get a clearer picture of whether or not your trading strategy is really working or not.

For the beginning, an investor should remember these basic guidelines.

- Pick a maximum of 50 stocks to trade, but invest them 1 at a time until they become second nature to you

- Choose the low stock prices, but not at the bottom, make sure they are at least above the $25 range

- Look for an average 30-day volume that is higher than 500,000 shares per day

- 25 of your shares should be set aside for long investments

- They should show increasing revenues and earnings
- Have a strong presence in their sector
- Have a moving average around 200
- Could even be following S&P Futures

- 25 of your shares should be used for short-term investments

  - These should show declining revenues and earnings
  - Have a weak presence in their sector
  - Have a moving average below 200
  - Could be following S&P Futures

Some Sectors That Have Been Favorable for Swing Traders

- Retailing

- Automotive

- Housing

These industries usually suffer when the interest rates are very high, however, when the economy begins to improve these industries will quickly recover.

You can also look at sectors based on the economy. Those in foreign countries will respond to different factors. You will have to consider currency fluctuations, political climate, and favorable or unfavorable events in the news.

When to Rotate

Once you have your sector choices for the market timing, you will need to know when to get out and switch to another sector. There are several methods to help you to decide exactly when it's the best time to rotate.

- When the market is on a downward slope

- When the fundamentals of your chosen sector start to go bad

- When you can find another sector with a higher potential for appreciation

- When you see that the sector is peaking and has met your target objectives

Top-Down Investing

With top-down investing the approach is a little different. You must look at the overall economy and then break down each of its components into smaller details. This means getting a good look at the global world scene, you can examine the different industrial sectors and choose those that have the potential of outperforming the market.

To do this you can use the macroeconomic variables like the trade balances, GDP, currency movements, inflation, and interest rates to help you to narrow down which sectors are most likely to be high performing.

Many investors get this information from hosted forums like the UBS CIO Global Forum held in Beverly Hills, California in 2016 to help them navigate the current economic environment. These venues address many of the macroeconomic factors that investors need to know. Open discussions on international governments, central banking, differing monetary policies, and what's happening in international companies can all have an influence on how a sector is responding into the market.

List of Sectors You Might Want to Consider

- Consumer Discretionary

- Consumer Staples

- Energy

- Financial (including banks, insurances, and brokers)

- Health Care (including pharmaceuticals)

- Industrial

- Material

- Technology

- Utilities

- Automotive

Each of these sectors can be subdivided into even smaller sector groups.

Now that you have all of your information together, you can now narrow down your search and determine which sectors you will trade in when you plan to trade, and which stocks you will focus the majority of your interest in. Sector rotation sounds very simple here, but there are many factors that must be considered if you want to make this type of investment strategy profitable for you.

Chapter 3: The 4-Hour Chart

Using the 4-hour chart are another popular method often used by swing traders. There are quite a few good reasons why working with this chart is so appealing. First, it is a bit longer than the smaller 5-minute or 15-minute charts that do not give a full enough picture of what's really happening with the money. But it is just long enough for investors to get a pretty good picture of what's kind of movement is going on in the market. By using this type of chart, it is pretty easy to see just who is in control at any given time, the bears or the bulls.

With the 4-hour chart strategy, the idea is to tap into the prevailing trends and make the most out of them by using a combination of several different moving averages, support or resistance, volatility, and other tools. When used together, these can help you to maximize your profits while at the same time keep your losses down to a minimum.

With the 4-hour chart as your base, you can screen for potential areas where you might find trading signals. Your main goal here is to identify either an uptrend or a downturn and then follow its unique behavior.

This is usually done by using two different sets of moving averages; one will be a 34 period and the other will be based on the 55 periods. These are both numbers that can be found in the Fibonacci sequence. You will be able to determine if a trend is good for trading or not by analyzing the relationship between the price action and the moving averages.

To Determine the Uptrend

You will be able to identify an uptrend if you have observed any of the following conditions

- The price actions are higher than the two moving averages

- The price action remains above both moving averages

- If the 34 moving average is higher than the 55 moving average and remains high

- If the moving averages are sloping upward for the majority of the time on the chart

To Identify a Downtrend

For there to be a downtrend, the same conditions must be observed, but in the opposite direction.

- When the price action falls below the two moving averages

- The price action stays below the two moving averages

- The 34 moving average is lower than the 55 moving average and remains low

- The moving averages are on a downward slope for the majority of the time and continue to fall behind the trend

Your goal is to profit on the swings that follow in the direction of the trend. This means you must also look for retracements and enter the market at that point. Below are some basic guidelines that can help you to decide the best point to enter the market.

- A trend must be identified in the 4th hour with the moving averages meeting the criteria listed above.

- Wait for a retracement to begin and then watch for the price to move in the direction of the two moving averages.

- When you see the retracement has reached the area between the two moving averages, look at the 1-hour chart of possible entry points.

- Find the retracement trendline that is moving counter to the trend and has touched the trend line at least three times.

- In the 1-hour chart, look for a breakout where a retracement trendline has closed in the same direction as the larger trend.

- Enter when the breakout price closes past the trendline.

One of the advantages of this strategy is that the trends are much more easily identified on the 4-hour chart. In most charts the upswings will be seen with white, rising candles and downswings can be seen with black, falling candles. It should be pretty easy to see the difference.

As a swing trader, you need to be able to visualize these movements and compare them to the current market situation. This strategy works best when there is an up or down trend, but will work even when there is a sideways trend.

There is a bit of psychology involved this trading strategy too. When the market experiences a certain level of support, there are many buyers hanging on the sidelines just waiting to jump in at the moment it moves up or down. As a trader, it is important that you can identify the psychological marks and predict when others are prepared to join the party.

Timing

The 4-hour chart also makes it easier to figure out the right time to enter or exit the market. When it comes to swing trading, in addition to getting the direction right, you need to know when is the optimum time to get in or out. As a matter of fact, timing plays a major factor in how well you do.

You also need to be concerned about periodic counter movements. At times you'll notice the market may run as much as 30-50 points against your position, but you will still make a profit if you stay your course. This is one advantage that a swing trader has over a day trader, who could never afford those types of counter movements.

Swing traders can also turn a much larger profit for each position they take. Chances are you are more likely to gain the most profit from those unexpected movements rather than those you predicted. With this method, you will typically have several hours to decide on a specific entry point, so you can afford to wait until you've found the perfect time to take your position.

Setting your Stop-Loss Placement

While this is a very profitable way to make money with swing trading, it is not without risks. Therefore, it is very important that each time you set your position you also create your own stop-loss placement carefully. This will help you to reduce your exposure risk and keep you from bleeding money when things go wrong.

Stop-loss placement is not the most idealistic decision a swing trader needs to make but is likely the smartest. If you do not fully understand how to pick the right position to stop your losses you stand to suffer considerable consequences. It is the single most powerful weapon needed to manage your risks.

The general theory is that the stop-loss should be based on a specific level in the market. The price action should have breached that level as evidence that your trade was actually wrong. Ideally, you want to see that the price actually invalidated your view and has used fact-based evidence as proof in the form of a breach of support or resistance.

There are several different types of stop-losses you can put into place. They are there as a protection not just for you are losing but to help you to be aware of potential losing trades. There is a tendency, especially among new traders to hold onto losing trades for far too long. We see a price plunging and it is just human nature to hold onto them in hopes that they will rebound, no matter what the conditions really are. By having a stop loss in place, it reduces your exposure to risk and cuts your losses.

Before you can accurately place a stop-loss, you must first answer one question: "At what point is it determined that your trade is wrong?" To answer this you will need to go back to your analysis, which will tell you not only determine where to place your stop-loss but also what type of stop-loss you will need.

Hard Stop

This is the easiest stop-loss placement you can use. It is just a matter of placing a stop at a certain number of pips from your entry price. A pip is actually the smallest price movement that any exchange can make. So, if a price is set at four decimal places, the smallest change would be that of the last decimal point or 1/100th of 1%. This means that you must also factor in the actual movement in the market. More volatile markets will require larger pipes to be effective and less volatile markets will require a smaller number of pips to show that your decision may have been wrong.

Average True Range % Stop

Another type is the ATR% stop, which can be used in any type of market. It is often used to determine the average true range of a particular stock. This range measures the volatility of a stock over a set period of time. When the ATR is higher, it is an indication of a more volatile market, but a lower ATR shows less volatility. Using this measure to determine your stop point is a way of ensuring that your stop will not be static, but will be dynamic enough to change with the prevailing market conditions.

Multiple Day High/Low

This type of stop is a popular one for swing traders. When taking a long position, the stop would be placed at the point where the trader will expect the day's low to be. This will allow you to exit the position at the first point where the break below that point is reached.

Closes Above or Below Price Levels

You can also set your stops when the price closes above or below predetermined price levels. With this type of setup, there is no actual stop placed in your trading software, instead, you will have to close it manually when it reaches a specific point.

Which Markets are Best?

When it comes to swing trading there are certain markets that are much better with the 4-hour chart than others. Shares may be the first choice, but they are not always the most ideal for all traders. There are certain factors that are out of your control that can impact your ability to earn a profit.

For those traders that wish to avoid huge price gaps, the alternative is to trade in specific markets. Rather than focus on particular stocks to invest in, concentrate on a market as a whole. For example, for those who choose to trade the Dow Jones, they are investing in not a single stock but in 30 different companies. So, while a single share may struggle on a particular day it is much more difficult for the entire market to experience a major loss.

This will prevent there being extreme gaps in profit earnings when the markets are very volatile. It is important to point out that there is no guarantee that this strategy won't experience major losses; it simply lowers your overall risk of losses you might experience by focusing your energies on a single stock. So, which markets are the best?

Indices
Bonds
Currencies

When you focus your attention on these, you will see many correlations that you can gauge by following practical rules. For example,

- When the American markets start to rise, markets in the other parts of the world will also see an increase.

- If the US dollar sees an increase, other currencies will often go down

- When the dollar is strong, other commodities are often weakened.

Simply by following these basic rules, you are fully prepared to know when to enter and exit the market and what to expect.

Which Instruments Are Best for Swing Trading?

Exchange-traded funds are investment funds that are traded on an exchange. Even if you don't know anything about these ETFs, there is plenty of information online so you can learn about the pretty quickly.

The majority of ETF's have a pretty good liquidity so it should be relatively easy to sell your position when you are ready to exit. Some of the most popular ETFs includes SPT – Standard and Poor's 500, QQQ – NASDAQ, and GLD – Gold.

When you trade on the 4-hour chart you need to develop a good understanding of the different items that you come across when you do your analysis. While you may have already heard of some of these expressions, it is a good idea to review them again so that you start off on the right foot. When you are searching for a setup (a pattern found on the stock market chart) you need to know what each of these things means. Many of them are very simple and basic but it helps to understand them when you see them and use them in making your investment decisions.

Support and Resistance

Look for support and resistance. These are some of the most powerful characteristics you can find when you're analyzing a market chart. These are usually found when you are doing your technical analysis.

Support is found when a price level appears at the point where the market repeatedly turns upward. This is the point when buyer interest increases. The more buyers in a market the higher the price will be.

Resistance is just the opposite. It is the point when the price level turns downward indicating that there are more sellers in the market. These push the prices down.

The reason why these points are so crucial is that, in some markets, a larger investor will only buy in when the price hits a certain point. While we can't all manipulate the market like this, knowing when these points happen can help you to buy in at the same point and reap the same profits.

As a swing trader, being able to recognize these pivot points could be one of the most profitable strategies you can have at your disposal. It will allow you to buy at the support level and sell at the resistance level for a steady stream of income.

Double Top and Double Bottom

Another pattern you will see on the charts is the double top and the double bottom. The double top pattern can usually be identified by an 'M' on the chart. It is viewed as an indication of an intermediate or sometimes a long-term price reversal. There will be two bullish attempts to push the price up past the resistance levels with two failed attempts to break through the threshold.

This pattern usually appears at the end of a long and extended uptrend. After reaching a specific high, the price will make a significant drop in value and create a trough before another attempt to break through to the new high. The second peak appears to be reaching the first peak, but is usually with a lower volume of trade. It's a sign that the bulls have lost confidence in the fight. The price drops again and the bears will take control.

This is considered to be a bearish chart pattern and is confirmed only when the price breaks at the low point of the trough. Traders can find this by looking for a high volume breakdown and then enter with a short position to take advantage of the reversal.

Ideally, you want to calculate the distance between the two peaks and the trough and then subtract the result from the lowest point of the trough to find the right point of entry for your trade.

The double bottom pattern is exactly the opposite and can be recognized as a 'W' on the charts. It gives you a good picture of a drop in a particular stock, then an attempt to rebound, followed by another drop to almost the same point before it rebounds a second time.

To trade on a double bottom, the closing price can be found on the second rebound and is almost to the previous high of the first rebound. You'll see an increase in volume combined with the fundamentals that give evidence that the market conditions are in agreement with the reversal. Trade long in this environment and enter at the top of the price point of the first rebound and set your stop at the second lowest.

The best way to trade on a double bottom is to stay abreast of the kind of news that would influence your stock. The more you know about what's going on and what factors are influencing buyer's decisions is to keep on top of the media and make sure that you know what's about to happen before it actually does.

Breakouts

Another pattern you need to be able to identify are the breakouts. These occur when the price moves outside of the support and resistance levels along with a large increase in volume. Those who trade on a breakout position usually enter long right after the stock price breaks above the resistance level. They can enter a short position when the price breaks below the support.

It is important to note that once a breakout occurs volatility tends to increase as the price is moving beyond a known parameter. Breakouts are found in all types of markets and generally represent the most explosive price movements.

When trading on a breakout, keep in mind the support and resistance levels. The more times a stock price has touched on these areas, the stronger these levels become. That means that the longer these areas have been at work, the better the result will be when the price finally breaks.

Choosing your entry point is pretty basic when you're trading with a breakout. Once the price is set to close above the resistance level, you can take a bullish position and when it closes below the support level you can take a bearish position.

Flags

Once a trend movement becomes stronger you will begin to see consolidation on the chart. The market will seem like it has stalled for a short period of time and then it will continue on following the prevailing trend. Sometimes this lack of movement is referred to as a 'trend continuation pattern.' It looks sort like a flag on the charts with the previous uptrend forming the pole and the short bursts of consolidation taking the shape of the flag.

When a flag formation is reached, traders can speculate on whether or not the trend will continue. These are great opportunities for a trader to speculate on both sides. There are bullish as well as bearish flags so there is an opportunity on both sides.

If you can play the flags just right, you can typically earn a pretty good risk-reward ratio. These appear frequently on the 4-hour chart, which makes it the perfect tool to use with this strategy.

Chapter 4: Trading Fakeouts

There is no doubt that talking about the market is much easier than actually doing it. With so many factors to consider it's no wonder that many people end up giving up after a time. Every trader needs their own body of algorithms, formulas, and strategies to help them navigate the sometimes murky waters of the trading game.

Those new to trading may be surprised to discover that everything you see on a chart is not always as it appears. There are often tricky characteristics that have been manipulated without the best of intentions. These are sometimes referred to as 'fakeouts' or 'feints.' Being able to identify them can be instrumental in helping you to avoid pitfalls and dangers that can easily overtake a newcomer and leave you helpless.

It is true that the same patterns on charts are repeated over and over again. These can usually be identified when you perform a technical analysis, but even then it may not always be clear.

To avoid being caught in a fakeout it helps to get a clear understanding of what it is. A fakeout (feint) can be described as a situation where the trader takes a position in anticipation of an expected price movement, but that movement never actually happens. Instead, the asset moves opposite of the trader's position.

To avoid this happening, it is recommended that you always use more than one indicator when making trading decisions. As you gain more experience in trading, you'll find that those traders who are most successful even rely on four or more indicators before they commit to a decision.

How to Spot a Fakeout

These fakeouts can occur anywhere, at any time, and in all types of markets so it pays to know just how to spot them when they appear. Below is a list of tips that can help even the beginning trader to identify fakeouts and avoid them.

One of the best ways to identify a true fakeout is by studying the charts of legitimate trends so you can learn how to recognize how price movements really do develop. You'll be able to see this in the candlestick pattern on the chart.

If there is a sudden rise in the market, you should be able to identify only white candles on the chart. Black candles appear when there is a downtrend. In these markets, you'll find that there is a loyal following. With these types of stocks, it is pretty easy to predict movements so it won't be easy for a large trader to get in and manipulate the prices.

Once the trend has reached its target, the market generally calms down and the volatility decreases. After that, it moves sideways for a period of time. It appears to be meandering aimlessly without forming any clear direction as if it were resting. In this scenario, all traders seem to have come to an agreement on the expected price point.

This scenario usually occurs when there is an expectation of big news relating to the stock. Reports of labor market disputes, major economic changes, or interest rate adjustments can often have a big impact on how the market will perform. It is the trader's responsibility to identify the validity of the movements and if he should anticipate more movement in a specific direction. However, if there is nothing happening in the market, no big news reports on the horizon, or no other indication of a change in price, you should probably assume it is a fakeout.

Traders can manipulate markets easier when there is not a lot of volume going on. They understand that there are many people sitting on the sidelines waiting for a signal for them to jump in and if he has enough money he can set up a fakeout pretty easily and then he can come in and reap the benefits.

By setting up a breakout, for example, traders will easily jump into the fray anticipating a rise in price. However, the trader who initiated the breakout immediately reverses his position once the other traders have joined in, forcing them to close their positions with a loss.

To gain from being trapped in a fakeout, it is better to wait for a breakout and if it ends up being a feint, respond in the opposite direction. Fakeouts usually appear on the support and resistance levels so you should be able to identify and predict certain price movements. Many traders are often caught at this point as it is a common rule of thumb to buy at support levels and sell at resistance levels.

Trading the Fakeout

Once you know how to identify a fakeout, you should prepare a strategy that will allow you to make the most out of the experience. This is what more experienced traders do. Rather than accept a loss as newbies often do, by applying a few basic rules you can turn that potential loss into a possibility for profit.

- Find the consolidation zones in your chart so you can determine the range the price is moving in.

- Draw trend lines on the chart so that they are more visible. Look for a minimum of two contacts with the trend line.

- Avoid this range and wait, hold your position until you see if the breakout is successful or not. If it fails, it is a fakeout.

- If it is a fakeout, open behind the breakout but in the opposite direction. If the closing price still falls outside of the range, hold your position. It could turn out to be a successful breakout.

- Look for range support for the price target when making short trades. Look for range resistance if you're planning on making long trades.

- Make sure you place your stops above or below the fake candle to prevent major losses.

- Aim for a 1:2 ratio. For example, if the distance to the stop is 50 pips, your target price should be twice that.

Identifying Patterns

Fakeouts can appear in a variety of patterns and can be found in all kinds of market situations. You can usually spot them on technical chart points because those that create them are well aware of the number of investors looking for those points to establish entry positions. As a trader, you need to be able to spot these quickly to avoid getting caught in the trap. If you are smart and can make good decisions, you can do quite well if you follow the pattern of those sharks and reap some of their spoils in the process.

Flags

Technical analysts prefer to create this pattern with two trend lines, keeping the small consolidation period contained in a narrow channel. The normal reaction is to expect the trend to move upwards, which would happen at the break of an upper channel line giving traders the buy signal to start another wave upward.

But with a fakeout, the opposite will happen first, triggering a sell signal. This will cause a slip in the price rather than an increase trapping those who were following the trend just a little too closely.

The smart trader will come in at a very low price and create a better risk-reward ratio, by monitoring this development more closely a nice windfall will be created for him or her.

Triangles

Triangles are another pattern you might observe a fakeout in. Normally, triangles are part of a continuation pattern where the analyst expects a breakout in the same direction as the trend. With a triangle fakeout, a swing trader could take a short position.

Market participants would expect the triangle to be a continuation of the trend and that it would resolve downward. They would assume that there was a start of an upward breakout, which would be a mistake. You will be able to identify this trick the moment the price appears to move in the wrong direction.

Channels

Channels are another way to create a fakeout on the charts. After the analyst has identified a trend he will look for a parallel trend line and connect the highs. Traders will naturally place their stops above the upper line if they plan to trade short or below the support line if they plan to trade long. Top traders are already aware of this move and will place larger orders that will perform in the opposite direction of the intended trend. If they can get over the top, they push the prices upward and will keep pushing until their short orders are executed, thus creating a flood of sell orders. This will force the price back down and back into the channel. The best traders should recognize this move and follow suit, adding to the trend.

As a trader, make sure you wait for the actual fakeout before you get in. It's a good idea to wait until the stops have all been fished out before you enter your position in the channel. This will give you a stronger confirmation as long as you trade in the same direction of the fakeout.

Chapter 5: Momentum Trading

Momentum traders look for acceleration at a stock's price before they enter the market. Once they have identified the momentum, they will take their entry positions with the expectation that the momentum is going to continue to follow that trend. Their method of trade is very similar to those who trade trend channels, but momentum traders are more likely to base their decision on short-term movements rather than on the fundamentals. This type of trading is not always easy and for that reason is more likely to be practiced by more experienced traders.

Timing is a key factor when you're momentum trading. Traders will set their entry points based on the speed of the stock movements and for that reason are much more interested in what's happening in the news at any given point in time. They look for those stocks that are moving to high volumes in reaction to such reports.

To be a momentum trader you have to have a keen sense of concentration and have the ability to stick with it until the target has been reached. Those who are not disciplined enough will usually lose out in this type of trade. The moves often happen very quickly and their timing has to be absolutely spot-on.

Screening Stocks for Momentum Trading

When looking for potential trades your focus should be placed on the search for trends. Once you find the trends, look to see if there is a strong movement in a specific direction. These movements must be accompanied by a high volume and have lasted over an extended period of time. There are several ways to find these types of trends.

Some traders look at daily watch lists or are continuously monitoring news reports, message boards, or brokerage apps for the latest news that will trigger a high volume trend.

They will look at stock volume as well. Since their interest lies in the momentum of a trade, the volume will be a major factor to consider. If they notice more buyers than sellers in the market, the price will rise and more trades will happen.

They will look closely at resistance levels. After they identify the stock trend and its direction, they will search out stocks that are already testing their resistance levels. If they find one that breaks the resistance it is considered a good candidate for momentum trading.

Technical indicators can also help to identify a break in resistance. Momentum traders are more concerned with moves based on a price trend if the stock has passed its point of resistance rather than the traditional buy at the bottom and sell at the top strategy. Once they enter they will stay in the trade until they have reached their target profit amount or hit their stop-loss point.

Short Squeeze

A well-played short squeeze can give an investor quite a bit of profit. Investors look for heavily shorted stocks so they can maximize their potential for gains.

A short squeeze happens when a stock has a high proportion of short interest as opposed to the overall float. When the value of a stock that is heavily shorted begins to increase, anyone who is trading short starts to lose a substantial amount of money. To cover his position, the investor will have to buy shares in the marketplace. Normally, this action won't have an impact on the price unless there is an excessive amount of short interest in the stock. When that happens, the stocks become flooded with too many of these purchases. The knee-jerk reaction of most traders is their stop-loss positions. These investors will switch positions to become long, pushing the stock price even further along forcing more short positions to close.

Another great way to identify a potential short squeeze is by looking for opportunities to play one. These can be seen when there is a large short percentage of float. One of the best places to look for these is on the NASDAQ. The higher the interest in the 'short' the greater the potential.

You can also check the daily volume. Once you are pretty sure that you know the number of shares being traded on an average day, look for some of the benchmarks that indicate an above average volume of movement in the stock. Take the short interest and divide it by the average daily volume. When there is a higher value for the number of days it is usually an indication that it is a longer squeeze in play.

When you are ready to trade in, ensure that the price is on an upward trend with a bullish push behind it. When everything falls into place, and you are in a long position, ride the wave looking for signs of a pullback.

In this type of trade, it is important to watch the chart closely. Look for the same trends you found when you identified the squeeze, but moving in the opposite direction. The volume will begin to spike as the price runs up after people begin to vacate their short positions. This would be a perfect example of watching a short squeeze as it plays out.

Conclusion

Thank you for making it through to the end of 'Swing Trading Strategies: Learn How to Profit Fast With These 4 Simple Strategies,' let's hope it was informative and able to provide you with all of the tools you need to achieve your goals whatever it may be.

There are many ways one can invest in the stock market, but swing trading seems to be one of the most popular. It doesn't have all the stress of the day trader and you have the ability to take your time as you navigate the market. This could be a very valuable tool when it comes to learning how to trade on the stock market.

The good news is that while in this book, we spent the majority of our time focusing on stocks, the techniques and strategies included here can easily be used in other areas as well.

So, whether you prefer to invest in the Forex, currencies, or even cryptocurrencies, the charts, and graphs referred to can all be analyzed in a very similar way.

Even though this book is contained in a very small package there is a lot of information here. It is not likely you will remember it all in one passing so keep it near you as you begin to navigate the market and use it as a reference from time to time. You can also enhance your learning by doing additional research on reputable sites online. No one knows everything there is to know about trading so if you decide to pursue this course of action, remember that you will always be a student.

Still, with the right attitude and diligent application of these strategies, you'll find you will enter the market with a little more confidence than before. As you start, make sure that you start with small trades first, and build up from there. With each success, I'm sure you'll be eager to try more and more, but remember to exercise patience and don't go too deep in the waters until you're sure you can actually pull yourself back to shore when you need to just in case.

Always remember that stock trading is, by its nature, a highly risky venture where you are always in jeopardy of losing everything you put into it. Take your time and be sure about every move you make. Never enter the market without at least two ways to get out of it. Remember to leave your emotions at the door and simply follow the numbers, graphs, and charts and you'll end up trading with nerves of steel that will carry you a long way as a trader who practices swing trading.

Finally, if you found this book useful in any way, a review on Amazon is always appreciated!